OUR FOOD ALSO FEELS

What do animals for human consumption think about our treatments?

EMILIANO ROJAS PEDROSO

DEDICATORY

To farm animals, who deserve a life filled with love and respect. This book is dedicated to them, in the hope that we can create a more compassionate and just world for all creatures on Earth.

CONTENTS

ACKNOWLEDGMENTS

Dear readers, I would like to take this opportunity to express my sincere thanks for joining me on this journey through the pages of this book, which tells the lives of six animals raised on factory farms. It's an honor and a privilege to be able to share with you these stories full of emotions, learning and reflections.

What do animals intended for human consumption think about the life we give them?

As the animals that we're, we have come to realize that our lives are determined by humans. They've raised us, fed us, and eventually killed us to become food. Although we aren't able to communicate verbally, we wonder what thoughts might run through our minds if we could talk to humans. What could we say to them? What questions could we ask them? What statements could we make about them?

If we could talk, we might ask them why they treat us the way they do. Why do they lock us in small cages, feed us a diet that isn't natural for us, and force us to live in an unhealthy environment? Why do they kill us in such a violent and inhumane way?

We could assert that our life and well-being matter as much as that of any other living being, including humans. That we deserve to be treated with respect, compassion, and dignity. That we deserve a life free of suffering, pain, and fear.

We could also ask them questions about their own diet. Have they ever wondered if they really need to eat so much meat? Have they ever considered the environmental and health impact of their diet on the planet (which is also our home) and on other people? Have they ever put themselves in our shoes and considered how they'd feel if they were raised to be eaten?

In short, although we can't speak, it's possible that, as animals intended for human consumption, we have many questions, dissertations, and assertions to make to humans. Perhaps if we could communicate, we could come to a mutual understanding and find a way to coexist in a more just and equitable manner.

It's time to get the other side of the story, from the perspective of a chicken, a cow, a sow, a lamb, a rabbit, and a female salmon.

Chapter 1.

Victor, the chicken

Hi, I'm Victor, a chicken raised on a farm for human consumption, and I'm going to tell you my story.

My arrival at the poultry farm was quite confusing. Suddenly, I found myself in a strange place surrounded by other unknown chickens who were just as terrified as I was. Most chickens my age don't survive in this environment, as we're crowded into small spaces and can't move our wings freely.

I don't know if this is good luck for us, though, as there are other male chicks that don't even make it here and are suffocated or crushed because they prefer females (males can't lay eggs). Therefore, they're considered unusable for this industry. So I don't know if I was lucky or unlucky to get here. To make matters worse, our lights almost never go out, which means we can't get enough rest. So we're kept in a state of alertness and latent stress.

My relationship with other chickens is limited, as the space we're given is very small and we can only be close to each other when crowded together; most of us are too busy trying to survive, but some chickens fight and peck to be the leaders of the group.

One of the things that terrifies and disgusts me the most is that I often have to live next to the corpses of other chickens, who leave them here to rot and never pick them up.

The humans who take care of us are strangers; they treat us as objects, not as living beings with emotions. They beat us, step on us, and throw us, resulting in fractures and injuries. Every time we go to eat, some chickens are randomly selected and taken out of the cage; they never come back. I know what happens, and I know deep down that this is my fate too.

I wonder if humans realize that we're living beings, not just food. I'm not afraid of them, but I don't trust them. They're too cruel, and I have the impression that they enjoy it.

The food they give us is insufficient for our needs; it isn't fresh and is made to make us fat faster. In fact, thanks to this accelerated fattening, our bones suffer fractures because they can't resist the abnormal weight of our muscles.

So basically, we're unable to move due to our excessive weight. For example, it's difficult for me to get to the feeders and drinkers because it isn't easy to move with this weight, and many suffer from fractures in the legs or wings, either because of the weight, being kicked, or crowding against each other.

Another major problem we suffer from is heart attacks. Because of our abnormal weight, we're very prone to having problems of that kind. So it's very common that, in a quiet moment, a chicken will start to convulse and die. That's very scary and stressful for me; it's a horrible way to die. It's also very traumatic for us as spectators and it shocks the environment.

You never get used to seeing others die in front of you, even though it's happened many times. It still produces the same fear as it did in the beginning.

Most of us are sick and aren't treated properly; we just get large doses of antibiotics in our water. I know because the taste of the water is different, and it tastes horrible. But in this heat and at this weight, I need to drink a lot of water, so I have no choice.

There isn't any space for us to run or exercise to stay healthy. We're fed food containing hormones and other chemicals that make us grow faster, which causes us pain and makes us feel sick. In other words, I'm fed a diet that focuses on rapid growth and not on my health and well-being.

Additionally, I live on my own excrement. The floor is completely wet with excrement, and all of that creates ammonia that burns our skin. So when I want to rest and lie on the floor, I'm aware that I'm also hurting myself. Resting is not recommended in this place either. And it gets worse if you have wounds on your skin. The burning is indescribable, sometimes you just give in to the pain and decide to rest a little.

Our plumage is also affected. With all that ammonia and dirt, the feathers don't develop properly, and we're much more exposed to the harmful environment. My feathers are white, but here they look rather brown or dirty, full of excrement.

I'm a living being with emotions and feelings, and I deserve a dignified and respectful life. Instead of being treated with compassion and care, I'm forced to live in extremely stressful and unnatural conditions, surrounded by other chickens in a crowded space with no access to natural light or fresh air. That is right, we rarely see sunlight. The only light we know is from the huge light bulbs that are almost always on, increasing the heat in this place and turning it into something akin to hell. Not to mention the air, it is impregnated with ammonia. It's almost impossible to breathe. It even makes my eyes water because of how intense it is.

My life of confinement is boring and

monotonous. Yet, I've never thought of running away because I don't know where to go, and I have nowhere to go. I clearly know what my future is, and I've resigned myself to my fate. If I could change anything in my life, it would be to have more space to move around and play with other chickens in a more natural environment.

I'd like humans to see us as living beings and not just as food. Because what if we did to them what they do to us? Wouldn't they at least ask us to show some mercy? That's all I ask. For example, I could have lived up to ten years under natural conditions, but here I'm sure I will not live past 42 days.

I feel deeply saddened and frightened at the thought of my inevitable fate. It isn't fair that my life has to be sacrificed to satisfy human appetite. I often wonder if there is any way to escape my fate, but sadly I know I have no choice. I'd like them to consider the pain and suffering we experience as animals raised exclusively for human consumption and to value our lives as much as that of any other creature on the planet.

I'd like to be allowed to live without being bred to be killed and eaten by humans. I'd like to appeal to their empathy to have compassion for my life and the lives of other animals bred for human consumption. But I know that won't happen. It's just utopia and foolishness of my mind clinging to hope when I know I won't have that chance. Maybe when you read this, I won't be on the farm anymore.

I hope my story generates reflection in those who read me and that they may see animals as I do in a different way. I hope they wonder if there is a way for us to be raised in a more humane and sustainable manner. Animals deserve to be treated with respect and compassion. Chickens, along with fish, are the most abused animals on the planet.

"What would happen if another species that considered itself superior to humans did to them what they do to us?" - *Victor, the chicken.*

Chapter 2.

Linda, the cow

Hi, I'm Linda, a cow who has lived her whole life in a factory farming barn. My arrival here was traumatic, as I was separated from my mother at a young age, which left me with a void in my heart that I've never been able to fill.

Then, when I gave birth to my daughter, she was taken away from me a few days later, which left me devastated and deeply saddened. I don't know where my daughter ended up, but I imagine she's in some other barn, far away from me, in the same or worse condition than me. I had machines attached to my udders to extract the milk that belonged to my daughter, and although I was in physical pain, my emotional pain was much worse.

I've been inseminated several times against my normal reproductive cycles; humans care that I can give birth so I can keep producing milk, but that makes me weaker every day, makes me prone to more diseases, and my milk, as marketed, isn't as healthy as they say because of all the hormones that go into it.

All my children have been taken away from me. I live in overcrowded conditions, confinement, and multiple mistreatments. My relationship with other cows is minimal, as we're all in the same conditions, trying to survive in this inhospitable and inclement place. In this barn, the space to move around is very small and quite dirty. I can barely take a few steps forward or backward, and I can't do any other activity beyond eating, drinking water, "resting," and of course giving milk and calving.

Overcrowding's a reality here, as there're many cows in the same space, and we all have to share the same hard, cold floor to rest on. The lack of space's a constant source of stress for me, because it makes me feel trapped and without any opportunity to move freely. This's especially worrisome because we cows are animals that're used to moving around in large green spaces and grazing.

In addition, the floor I'm standing on isn't natural; it's a cement and metal surface that causes pain in my legs, makes me feel uncomfortable all the time, and sometimes bleed.

Another problem in this barn is the lack of ventilation. The air is always laden with the smell of excrement and urine, something that's made even worse by the number of animals in the same space. This makes the air thick and difficult to breathe, and can also cause respiratory problems and illnesses in us.

One of the most stressful times of the day is when I'm taken to the machines that endlessly pump my milk and leave me very sore. The humans have no mercy; I suffer from lameness, which is a very common condition in all the cows that live in this place, but they don't seem to care, as they kick me and when I fall down they hit my face or my stomach to make me move and walk at the pace they want. Sometimes they've even used tweezers to make me move. Sometimes I'm so exhausted that I simply faint, and they twist my tail, which causes me deep pain, as it's a very sensitive area for our species.

Humans seem to enjoy this act of cruelty against us; they even laugh. I don't understand how one species can enjoy at the expense of the suffering of another, but they do. They even joke among themselves about the methods of torture they can inflict on us.

They don't treat our diseases; they let many

cows die of agony to save money and not spend on veterinarians. I've had to see many cows throughout my life suffer and die for hours and even days. One of the situations that shocked and shook me the most was when a cow couldn't give birth and her calf died inside her. They did nothing to help her; they just let her suffer with her dead calf inside, and she had to agonize painfully for days until her death.

When I see humans, I feel a mixture of fear, hopelessness, and dread because I know they have no interest in my welfare, but only in taking advantage of my flesh and milk. My reaction isn't one of joy or curiosity but of fear and distrust. Since I was a calf, I have been handled, manipulated, and mistreated by humans, always with one goal in mind: to get as much milk as possible from my body for their consumption and, at some point, my meat. For me, humans are the beings who have taken my children from me and made me suffer deeply throughout my life.

I don't understand why humans are so cruel to me and my female companions in confinement, and why they take our children, our bodies, and our lives mercilessly. To me, they're strange and highly dangerous beings, causing me pain, fear, and sadness.

In my mind, I cannot understand why someone can cause so much harm without caring about the suffering of another living being. They think that we're too stupid to realize what is happening; they think that we're unaware that we are going to be sacrificed. We aren't stupid, and we know what will happen to us. We just have no way to defend ourselves, and in their eyes, we have no rights.

About my life of confinement, I can only say that

it's a nightmare that has no end. The food they give me isn't enough to maintain my health, and the antibiotic shots I constantly receive make me feel quite sick. I wonder if they're aware that it will go into their bodies when they drink my milk or eat my meat.

The fact that I'm being fattened up to be killed and then eaten by humans is something that terrifies me deeply. I know that my death will be painful and merciless, and that my flesh will be used to satisfy the tastes of humans. And worst of all, I have heard that my skin will also be used to make handbags and other objects, which makes the picture that much crueler.

I think about my future with fear and sadness because I know I have no chance of escaping this place. Although I have sometimes thought about running away, it's only a thought to escape for a few moments from my reality. I know that this is practically impossible. So, I have accepted my reality, even though it hurts me to the core of my being.

My existence is limited to eating, producing milk, and fattening up to be slaughtered for human consumption. Throughout my life, I have seen other members of my species treated inhumanely. Some have even died due to the terrible conditions in which we live. I wonder if someday humans will realize the suffering they cause to animals like me, and if they will change their way of thinking and acting towards us.

I wish they could empathize with me and other animals living in these conditions. Why do they treat us this way? Don't we deserve to be treated as well as any other living being? I want my story to be told so that humans will question their actions and take action to stop this cruelty. We animals do not deserve to live in these inhumane conditions, to be treated as objects, and then to be killed en masse.

This wasn't the life I wanted to have for myself. I wanted a life in natural freedom, but that is no longer a possibility. I know that my existence is condemned and will be limited to suffering until the end. When you read these lines, I will surely have already gone to the slaughterhouse, and my meat will be found in some supermarket ready for sale. Or maybe it will be the next steak you eat. I hope that someday we will be valued for what we are: living beings deserving of good treatment.

"If cruelty could be transformed into energy, humans would be unrivaled." - *Linda, the cow.*

Chapter 3.

Isabel, the sow

I'm Isabel, a sow raised on a pig farm. My life has been a succession of suffering and exploitation. One of my first contacts with humans was when they cut off my tail without anesthesia when I was only a few days old. It was unbearable pain, and I asked for help, but they didn't seem to care.

At three weeks old, I was separated from my mother and siblings and taken to a section where there were many more pigs from different mothers. I felt very worried and troubled being separated from my siblings and not being able to find them in the midst of so many pigs, while some humans were yelling and kicking us. Since then, my life has been a constant struggle to survive in a cramped and tremendously dirty space.

At puberty, I was inseminated and taken to an uncomfortable "gestation and maternity" cage where I could not move, not even turn around. I stayed there for two and a half months, surrounded by other sows in the same situation. After giving birth, I was kept immobilized in the "maternity cages" (iron frame that separates the sow from the offspring) for several weeks, unable to give love to my children and only lying down for them to suckle.

My children were taken from me at three weeks, just as I had been taken from my mother. Then, this same process repeated over and over again, and each time I became weaker and more exhausted.

My life as a sow on a farm has been marked by overcrowding, confinement in cages, excrement, and bad smells. I wonder if humans realize the suffering they inflict on us or if it is part of their process. The other sows around me are just as stressed and often behave aggressively and wildly, so I don't even have friends or anyone to socialize with. We are just a bunch of living beings suffering together.

There are no distractions in my life, only sadness, suffering, and mistreatment. A sow like me lives between two and three years in these conditions, while in natural conditions, I would live at least fifteen years.

Diseases are becoming more and more common due to the massive exploitation to which we are subjected. The forced inseminations we suffer over time can cause severe prolapses, so it can be very common to see sows with the uterus or organs exposed, as our bodies aren't designed to have offspring so continuously.

Mastitis is another big problem that we almost never receive treatment for, and conjunctivitis and skin problems are also common due to the unhealthy environment we're forced to live in. We don't receive proper treatment because it's cheaper to keep us sick than to pay for proper veterinary care. Even in severe cases, they let us agonize to death or kill us with blows, hammering, or any other creative way they can think of. In addition to giving offspring and meat, we can also be victims of their sadism.

The stress burden to which I'm subjected is so intense that I've reached the point of breaking and grinding my teeth against the metal bars of my cage, which is more like a kind of prison. I feel locked up, frustrated, and sometimes find it hard to recognize myself. That's been the only way I've found to deal with the despair and overwhelm I feel.

The food we're given isn't very tasty, in fact, it's mostly artificial, designed only to keep us alive.

But it's all we have, and there's no other choice. Feeling hungry when you're breastfeeding or pregnant is agony (which is a big part of my life), so you have to eat that. I know humans see us as filthy, disgusting animals. Personally, I like to be kept clean. However, I have no choice but to do my biological needs in my tiny cage and live with that.

Do humans realize the suffering they subject us to? Why do they find pleasure in mistreating us and making us suffer to death? How can anyone justify this massive and ruthless exploitation of animals?

I know that I'll soon be inseminated for the seventh time, and that this will possibly be my last litter. At least I won't bring my children to suffer in this cruel world anymore. My reproductive capacity has diminished, and my life of mass exploitation is coming to an end.

That means I'm no longer profitable. After that, I'll be taken to the slaughterhouse to be killed in a cruel and inhumane way. I'm not totally certain about the specifics of my death, but judging by the kind of life I've been given, I don't think I'll be given a quiet and peaceful death. That would be very naive of me, and naivety is no longer a quality that accompanies me in this life.

Although the idea of death scares me, I see it as my only way out to finally rest from life and be free from this prison. I've never had a day to enjoy, and I've never known freedom. I have no hope of doing so. I don't know what it's like to breathe fresh air or receive sunlight, and I never will. But thinking that way about my life doesn't make me a coward, just a victim who, deep down, is waiting with longing and uncertainty for that day when it all ends. I'm just a living sentient being whose will to live has been broken. Why would there be any sense or reason to cling to this life? Exactly, none.

What about respect and justice for animals? Do humans really need to eat so much pork? As a sow on a farm, I feel used and without a personality of my own. My only function in life is to give birth to offspring that I can't see grow up and finally be sold for parts. Because some profit they must get from me in the end, as there doesn't seem to be enough for them.

But I want humans to know that I am more than that. I deserved a dignified life free of suffering. I won't ask for compassion for myself, because I know they don't have the capacity to feel it. And to their ears, I would only be the squeals of a pig and a dying animal. But I would like at least my children, for whom I'm possibly just one more animal in the melee, to have a better life than the one I had and not suffer as much as I did.

Although, being very honest, I doubt it.

Perhaps, upon reading my story, you'll say things like "Oh, poor little Isabela!" I'm not looking for your pity, I demand your respect. If you aren't willing to do anything to improve the living conditions of my species, then you're no better than those who mistreat us. You're simply a silent, cowardly accomplice.

Don't misunderstand my words. I'm not speaking from hatred or rancor. I'm simply telling the truth as it is, something your kind should learn from us instead of speaking from the perspective of political correctness, which leads to inaction. At least in the midst of my exhaustion and despair, I don't succumb to fear, and I don't stay silent. I choose to squeal!

I know that when you think of a pig, you probably imagine a free and happy animal on a farm, as they're often presented to us as adorable and cuddly. However, that only represents 1% of our reality. It's time for you to know the truth behind the other 99%.

I ask you to break away from the misconception that pigs are cuddly creatures living on happy farms. Instead, I invite you to reflect on the reality of most pigs and consider making changes in your consumption and lifestyle to support a more ethical and fair food industry because, in the end, this industry responds to a wild demand that comes from your plate.

"It's naive to expect a species to provide something that is simply not in its nature to provide." - *Isabel, the sow.*

Chapter 4.

Vicente, the lamb

Hello! I'm Vicente, a lamb raised on a sheep farm. I was born in a dark, dirty, and ugly place controlled by humans; the only time I could feel my mother's love and warmth was when she breastfed me for the first and last time before I was separated from her, although she didn't look so good to be honest, she looked exhausted, and signs of mistreatment were visible. She made me promise to be a brave lamb, that despite the adversity and fear of the moment, I'd be strong.

As the humans separated me from my mother, I don't deny that I felt scared, but I had promised her that I had be brave, and so I did, even with tears in my eyes. When the humans pierced my ear to put a label, I was one of those who resisted the least, although it hurt me too much, I tried not to be so startled, since those who did so received blows. Then I understood that my mother was preparing me for a difficult and cruel world, her words at that moment ceased to be hopeful and became resignation for me.

After being marked with that label, I was taken together with other lambs to a gigantic place where there were many lambs of different ages, and they were separated by the color of their labels. This whole stressful situation happened in less than an hour, with shouting in the background and constant banging to speed up our steps.

I and others like me were put in a place where we were cramped together and didn't have space to move, in fact, we were on top of each other. The place was quite dirty and full of our excrement and urine, with strong odors and little ventilation, besides being very dark and with a feeling of desolation despite the noise of so many animals together.

In that hostile environment, I had to struggle to survive, and I was fed with a rather unpleasant artificial milk that didn't compare at all with my mother's milk. That milk made us grow and gain weight quickly, so you can imagine that the overcrowding was worse, and basically, we had to fight to eat as if we were savages. The weaker ones couldn't eat and got sick, and some died. The artificial milk caused intestinal problems for me and the others, which worsened the hygiene of the environment.

A few days after being in that place, me and the other lambs had our tails cut off with scissors. It was very painful and traumatic, especially because the procedure was done without anesthesia. I could only cry and try to stand up because if I lay down, the others would step on me.

At that moment, I couldn't help but feel fear and pain, and I longed for my mother's presence, even though I knew I would never see her again. I only pretended to be brave, but I was terrified. Some lambs became infected after the cut, but the humans didn't care, and some had serious consequences. Fortunately, my wound healed very quickly.

In that place, there was no way to get distracted, let alone have friends, as I was basically struggling to survive every day. I couldn't sleep much either because it was almost impossible. While I was there, I learned to distinguish the different types of lambs that shared that huge place and understood the reason for the labels on our ears.

For example, I'm a suckling lamb, and I've got a blue tag, which means that I'm only fed milk, and we're usually slaughtered at 45 days of life to obtain soft and light-colored meat, much appreciated by humans (I know because I heard them talking about it, although they think we don't understand them because we don't react, but the truth is that there's nowhere to escape). Then there are the recentals, they live between 45 and 100 days, their first 45 days they only drink milk like me, but then they're given a kind of grass and cereals. Finally, there are the Easterlings, they live more than 100 days and are slaughtered at Easter, a celebration much loved by humans.

Every time I saw humans walking around my space, I felt a deep fear that completely invaded me. In their presence, I couldn't help but feel vulnerable and helpless, as if I was exposed to some kind of imminent danger. I knew that sooner or later it'd be my turn to be next on their list of victims, and the very thought made me shiver.

Even though I couldn't communicate with them verbally, I sensed there was something wrong with the way they were treating me. They seemed to enjoy my suffering, my pain, my sadness, or at least they didn't care at all.

I never knew what life was like outside of that place, but I was sure that anywhere was better than that. From my small space where I spent most of the day locked up, I often wondered if there was something beyond those walls.

I imagined what it'd be like, but that was just a fantasy, a pipe dream in a world that had been taken from me since birth. So the thought of what it could be made me even sadder, sometimes imagination isn't such a good ally.

The day I turned 45 days old, the humans came for all of us blue labels, and with screams, blows, and kicks, they dragged us out of there. I knew my time had come and there was nothing to be done, but I was terrified. Then they tied us by our front legs in groups and weighed us, as if we were bunches of bananas. They don't see us as living beings but as a pile of meat.

After that, they threw us on a truck, so it was only a matter of hours. We arrived at a rather narrow place, and they started to unload us violently and make us walk. Many of the lambs seemed to have gone crazy; the fear was in their eyes, and it was no wonder. I was able to stay calm and keep walking down this narrow hallway between pushes, even though inside I was fading.

But it's very difficult to be calm when you know what's going to happen to you, and you can see in the distance how humans hang lambs by their hind legs and pierce their throats with a knife, while leaving them to bleed to death. The screams of despair and terror here are horrifying, both from those being killed and from us, the spectators who are slowly walking towards the same end (they think we don't understand what's happening).

My legs are shaking and my heart's pounding, but there's no escape, I knew that from day one. I try to be brave and think that there's no other option. After all, it'll only be a moment of pain, and then I won't feel anything anymore. I'm trying to see it that way, even though I wanna run away because I'm afraid of dying this way, it's not fair, but there's no justice for living beings like me.

I don't understand what's the need for humans to torture us in this way. I'm just a baby, and I feel, and I'm sure that I don't deserve this. Why do they think they've the power to deny me the opportunity to become a ram or a sheep in the case of females? Do they do the same to their babies?

By the time you read this, I'll be hanging by my legs, probably dead. I hope it was as quick and painless as possible for me.

"Under normal conditions I could've lived up to fifteen years, humans only allowed me 45 days"
- *Vincent, the lamb.*

Chapter 5.

Héctor, the rabbit

Hi, hello! I'm Héctor, a rabbit raised on a rabbitry. I bet you've rarely heard that word, but it refers to a rabbit farm for commercial purposes. Unfortunately, they aren't pretty purposes, in fact, they're quite cruel. I'm sure you understand what I mean, and if you don't, you'll pretend to learn, anyway.

I don't know where to begin to tell you my story. What nerves! Maybe I should start from the day I found out I was being fed and then sacrificed. No, maybe I'm too strong to start. Or maybe, when I realized I wasn't mentally stable anymore after tearing off part of another rabbit's ear. I'm not sure, that makes me sound like an evil, unhinged rabbit.

Should I talk about the nasty things in this place? My illnesses? The wicked humans? I'm not sure. I'm sorry, I'm finding it very difficult to organize my thoughts. I think I'm very damaged after so much mistreatment, even though I'm innocent. Ah, that's it! Let's start from the time when I hadn't yet known cruelty, just when I was born.

Let's start, now let's start. I may sound a bit unbalanced, I know, but sometimes my head doesn't work quite right. My mental health's quite deteriorated, but don't worry about that, pay attention to the essence of my story.

I must say I remember everything very well, not to brag, but I have a good memory. Ironic, isn't it? It'd be better if I suffered from amnesia, but then I'd forget that I have to eat or I'm gonna be killed. It's definitely better to be aware of everything, even if I'm sometimes absent at times. Anyway! I'll concentrate.

I was born into a litter of twelve siblings. Yes, I know, rabbits are prolific creatures. We were in a very small cage, and my mom was trapped in there. Sadly, two of my siblings died just minutes after birth. Then the humans arrived for an inspection (that's when I learned about cruelty). They realized three of my siblings were very small and felt they wouldn't be useful for the purposes they needed. They'd basically be losses to the business, so they took them out of the cage and threw them in a dumpster, leaving them to their fate to agonize and die.

This was their standard procedure with other litters, it wasn't personal. This was all done as part of controlling excess production. As you can see, I've learned a few things in my short life.

I spent four weeks with my mom and siblings in a tiny cage. I must admit she wasn't particularly affectionate, looking rather sad and distant, although she did feed us. From the looks of her breasts, she seemed to have had several litters before us.

At the end of those four weeks, the humans separated us from her and took us and other rabbits to cages a little larger than my mother's, but crowded with rabbits. In my cage, there were ten of us in total.

I should mention that because the humans transported us in large groups in containers and randomly distributed us to complete the cages, I didn't coincide with my siblings in the newly assigned space. The humans don't seem to care much about the family thing, to them we're all the same.

My new cage mates and I were extremely scared and upset. We were basically strangers to each other, and having to be so close to them was uncomfortable. Most of us chose to isolate ourselves and avoid interaction for the first few days. Although the cage was more spacious than my mother's, there was nowhere to rest properly, as the floor was made of wire, and we were three feet off the ground so our droppings and urine would fall there and we wouldn't live on them.

However, they took a long time to clean the floor, which caused strong odors that attracted flies. It was extremely uncomfortable, but we had no choice but to put up with it.

The wire floor of our cage was extremely uncomfortable and it was very hard on our feet. In addition, the space was so limited that we didn't have the freedom to run or move around without disturbing the other rabbits. Unfortunately, this was the same situation in the other cages. The atmosphere was dreary and gloomy, permeated with nauseating odors.

It's not nice, having your excrement and that of others as a lower floor.

One day, the humans took us out of the cages to mark our ears. This procedure was painful, as it consisted of clamping my ears with a kind of clip that engraved a number, and then they applied ink. It was without a doubt one of the most painful experiences I've ever had in my life. My ears are extremely sensitive, and that kind of damage caused acute pain. I remember emitting a shriek that I'd never heard from myself before, and so did everyone else. We were all terrified and in pain.

The confinement in which we live generates strange and irrational behaviors. Because of the stress we're under, it's common for us to attack each other.

It's happened to me on several occasions, it's

something that's considered normal in this environment. One day, without knowing what happened to me, I attacked one of my colleagues and bit his ear, tearing off a piece of it. Unfortunately, these types of situations are common and normal for all of us. I felt terrible because I didn't recognize myself, as I was never aggressive. In fact, I too am missing a piece of my ear. Violence and madness have become commonplace here. Cannibalism is a reality, and we're no longer as lovable as we seem.

Another major problem is untreated illnesses. Many of us have open wounds that don't heal, and we receive no care to heal them. We simply find ourselves getting more and more infected every day and with a lot of flies around us. It's really disgusting. Here, everything tends to get worse. A wound is a sign of prolonged suffering.

A common disease among us is pasteurella, a bacterium often associated with respiratory infections. It can cause coughing, shortness of breath, runny nose, conjunctivitis, painful abscesses on the neck or cheeks, and a feeling of lethargy or lack of energy. Unfortunately, we never received treatment for these illnesses.

One day, one of my cage mates became ill due to an open wound and couldn't feed anymore, as he'd lost all strength. The humans came and slammed him to the ground three times, without showing a shred of compassion or remorse.

As they conversed among themselves, I heard them say that this rabbit wasn't even fit to be eaten and wouldn't reach the weight required for slaughter. It was a terrible spectacle to witness how despite the blows, he continued to writhe on the ground. I was shocked and understood that my fate would be the same: to be eaten. That revelation broke me inside; I experienced an icy sensation that ran through my skin, I think that's what's known as pure fear.

Since then, I've experienced involuntary movements and I lose my sense of things regularly, something that's common to all of us here. No one's healthy, we suffer a lot and our brains seek to protect us somehow, pulling us out of our miserable reality. But sometimes, instead of beating us, they choose to break our necks, a quicker way to end our existence.

Humans instill in me an inordinate fear. I see them as perverse, ruthless, and calculating beings. Every time I perceive them, I feel that my heart's about to burst out of my chest, and I fear that my time has come.

This feeling accompanies me day after day, even when they only come to provide us with food. Have I already told them about the food? No, I don't think I have. The food they give us is unhealthy, full of calories and additives designed to make us fat quickly, which means less living space as we grow. In addition to feeding us, this food also causes problems with our bones, heart, and digestive system. I don't know if that can be considered food or rather poison.

Some of us have even lost our fur, living with exposed skin due to poor nutrition that prevents us from having a proper immune system. Because of this, we no longer look so adorable and cuddly, but rather nasty and scary. We're a bunch of rabbits with open wounds, infested with flies, bald, dirty, and somewhat disoriented or crazed, however you prefer to describe it.

I know what awaits me, as do many others here. We've overheard their conversations. It scares me, but it also comforts me, because I can't imagine spending much time in this place. I'll end up losing what little sanity I've left.

When we're ten weeks old, they'll take us to the slaughterhouse. Do you know how long I could live in a natural environment? Up to ten years. However, under the "care" of humans, only ten weeks. At least we get the same number. Isn't it ironic? I know it's not funny, but what else can I do besides laugh at my own misfortune?

Here's a spoiler of what's in store for me. When I turn ten weeks old and reach a weight of 'bout two kilograms, regardless of whether I'm sick or not, I'll be taken to the slaughterhouse. I'll be taken out of this cage in an abrupt and inconsiderate manner, without losing the habit of mistreatment. Once I arrive at the slaughterhouse, they'll hold my head and place it on an electric plate to stun me with around 80 to 110 watts. At least I'll be able to see the light for a moment (I joke), but I know this will supposedly render me unconscious. However, for larger rabbits like me, that voltage won't completely stun us, which means I'll be aware of what'll follow next.

I'll be hung by my hind legs, and a knife will cut my jugular vein, as I struggle to cling to life and bleed to death. I don't understand why I'd cling to this life, that's how damaged I am.

After that, they'll make cuts in my skin, cut off my ears, and easily strip me of my skin. Then, they'll proceed to remove my organs and viscera, and once they're done with me, they'll send me to refrigeration to then be sold in a supermarket, where they can prepare "delicious" dishes using the meat of a sick rabbit.

"In this place, common sense is as rare as a rabbit without scars. Fortunately, rabbit meat is low in fat, but they never mentioned that it's also full of traumas" - *Héctor, the rabbit.*

Chapter 6.

Susy, the salmon

Hello, my name is Susy, a female salmon raised in an industrial fish farm. My life has been very complex, marked by overcrowding and constant moving. I remember when I was just a fry, that's a baby, I lived in a rather small artificial pond surrounded by thousands of fish like me, where there was almost no space to move. It was a very traumatic place for me since I was only a few weeks old, and I didn't understand what was happening.

After a few weeks, they moved us to a new pond. For this, they used some nets and put us crowded in buckets with very little water to move us to that new pond. Really, that was a massacre, as many died crushed by others. The fear you feel is frightening because you have nowhere to go, but you also don't know what to do or where to flee because basically, I was a prisoner.

This move happened because we weren't fry anymore, and we were starting to be parr, something like teenagers or youngsters. The new pond was bigger, but considering that we had all grown up, the feeling of overcrowding was the same or worse. We stayed there for five horrible months, living without knowing why.

Then the same as the previous time was repeated, and we were transferred in the same dire and carefree conditions to a new pond (yet another massacre), with the difference that in this one, the water was salty. When I came in contact with that water, my eyes burned, and I felt burning in my scales since it was a very abrupt change. This process is called smoltification, and it's done to "adapt" to the salty water and prepare us for our new transfer. There we remained for five months.

All the ponds I'd been in had the same thing in

common: overcrowding. We had no place to swim, just to try to survive. The water quality was terrible, and there was almost no oxygen. It was almost like living on the edge of death in a state of constant and acute stress.

In addition, we lived and "swam" in our waste, as they rarely or almost never cleaned those ponds. For example, salmon that died crushed or sick decomposed there next to us, and also the remains of food (I'll tell you about food later). Basically, we were in a waste pond, with little light and murky water.

I didn't have the opportunity to create lasting friendships because we were constantly being moved around, so it was hard to match up with the same salmon again. One of the things that caused me the most stress was the fact that, as salmon, we're very orderly and have structures and social intelligence systems that allow us to organize ourselves in groups with established hierarchies. Well, all of this, we had to try to reset it every time we were moved to a different pond, so the chaos and commotion were constant and reigning.

So there comes a moment where you just try to see for yourself and make sure you live because it's not possible to organize yourself in the middle of a constant wave of changes and moves. Besides, many became aggressive and attacked each other, they even ate each other, all the product of stress and suffering because, believe it or not, fish also feel. We experience anxiety and pain. In fact, humans already have scientific proof of this, but they still treat us like things.

So it was very common to see other salmon with damage, untreated injuries, or even broken fins. In fact, I once had to fight because another salmon attacked me, fortunately at that time, they threw the "food" at us, and that dissipated any continuation of the confrontation.

The food, on the other hand, wasn't any less horrible than the overcrowding, basically tasteless, artificial, and heavily loaded with antibiotics that sometimes left me in a drowsy state. They do this to force us to grow unnaturally large in a short period of time.

Humans should know that so many antibiotics in my body will also end up in their stomachs, and eventually, they'll show resistance to antibiotics because, in a way, through us, they're manufacturing their own doom in an area where they've already advanced a lot.

Where was I? Ah, yes, the smoltification and the fact that they were going to move us to a new place (what a novelty!). Forgive me if sometimes I don't link or conclude my ideas well, but after so many antibiotics, suffering, and stress, I'm no longer the same, nor am I very sane.

Just when I thought nothing could get worse in my life, we were moved, but this time it wasn't to a pond, as that saltwater pond was an adaptation to live in floating cages in the sea. Yes, when you think that nothing can be worse with humans, they can take it to the next level. Every time I saw them, they gave me terror and despair because their presence isn't good for us. And here began the real horror and suffering.

After surviving a hectic transfer, where I was beaten and had to crush others to stay alive and not get buried at the bottom of the tank in which I was transported, we were thrown by the thousands into the floating cages in the sea. I'd never seen anything like it. They were huge, rather colossal, filled with more salmon like me, struggling and suffering to stay alive.

This was supposed to be our new home for the next twelve to eighteen months. Terror and hopelessness came over me because it wasn't only the overcrowding, the waste, the aggressiveness, but we'd have to deal with a plague: sea lice. Those parasites attached themselves to my skin, fed on my blood, and released their toxins that made me feel very sick and weak, and the other salmon as well.

In addition, these creatures reproduce quickly, and without sufficient presence of cleaner fish or natural predators, we were vulnerable, which opens the possibility for us to get sick more easily because the lice feed on our defense systems, the mucus.

Infections here are rampant, and it's quite an

unpleasant environment. You can see fish rotting away in life, and you know deep down it's happening to you too, just at a slower pace.

Many try to run away and just hit the cage many times, get injured, and possibly die. There's no escape. You're either killed by batteries, sea lice, or humans, but death is certain under these conditions. In a natural environment, I could've lived at least ten years. Here, I know I won't make it past two years.

When I reached my sexual maturity, the humans did one of the most painful things I've ever experienced. They took me out of the cage in the sea and took me to a pond, there they made a cut in my abdomen and started to extract my eggs manually, with their fingers. It hurt so much, and it was like agony; I think that at times I became unconscious from the pain. This was done to other females that they selected because we were in "good conditions," and to some males, in their case, they extracted their sperm; this in order to fertilize the eggs and produce new generations of salmon condemned to pain and suffering.

This means that my end is near, they'll kill me. I'm waiting for my death, which I'm sure will be slow and painful. I know that humans cut our gills and let us bleed to death, by asphyxiation, crushed (something very common in our lives), and many times we're beaten to death; we can't complain, options are what we have.

In fact, many times when they're removing our organs, we're still alive and we can feel everything, but that doesn't stop them; they're experts in torture.

I want you to know that the meat you're going to eat from me, besides being sick, is gray. It's not the color you think or see in your supermarkets, because we've been fed with synthetics that dye our meat. In natural environments, yes, it's the color "salmon," because that coloration comes from our diet. We eat crustaceans that contain a natural pigmentation called astaxanthin.

Today, there're food companies that offer color catalogs to salmon producers (i.e., my executioners), so they can choose the shade of salmon they want. Although they say it's purely aesthetic, think about this next time you eat salmon. Would you eat a salmon that you know is gray and they've artificially dyed its flesh to make it look attractive to you? Don't you think they're cheating you too?

"Just because we don't emit sounds of pain, does NOT mean we don't feel and are content with the treatment we receive" - *Susy, the salmon.*

To keep in mind

After delving into the stories of these six animals, you may feel moved and wonder what you can do to help improve the situation of animals raised for human consumption.

It's important to note that the goal of this book is not to criminalize meat consumption or blame, but rather to invite readers to reflect on how these animals are treated and to consider whether there are more humane and ethical ways to produce food.

The aim is not to judge, but to raise awareness and encourage consumers to make informed choices about what and how they eat.

We hope this book inspires you to reflect on your relationship with animals and that you can find ways to be part of the shift towards a more just and compassionate world for all living things.

About the author

Emiliano Rojas Pedroso was born in Colombia and graduated as a Social Worker from the Universidad Francisco de Paula Santander (Cúcuta). He's a passionate and sensitive defender of animal rights and a nature lover.

He has created this book as a space to give voice to those beings that are often forgotten in society. Through his writing, he conveys the importance of empathy and connection with all forms of life, inviting readers to reflect on their relationship with farm-raised animals and the impact our decisions have on them.

Visit the blog or write to the e-mail
emiliano01360@gmail.com